Our Amazing States™

New Hampshire
The Granite State

Robin Koontz

PowerKiDS press™

New York

To the road not taken

Published in 2011 by The Rosen Publishing Group, Inc.
29 East 21st Street, New York, NY 10010

First Edition

Editor: Amelie von Zumbusch
Book Design: Greg Tucker
Layout Design: Ashley Burrell
Photo Researcher: Jessica Gerweck

Photo Credits: Cover, pp.11, 17, 19, 22 (tree, deer) Shutterstock.com; p. 5 Kim Grant/Getty Images; p. 7 © Scott Smith/age fotostock; p. 9 © North Wind Picture Archives; p. 13 © www.iStockphoto.com/ Tom Tietz; p. 15 © Frank Siteman/age fotostock; p. 22 (bird) © www.iStockphoto.com/Ron Lacey; p. 22 (flower) © www.iStockphoto.com/Anneclaire Le Royer; p. 22 (Franklin Pierce) Hulton Archive/Getty Images; p. 22 (Alan Shepard) SSPL/Getty Images; p. 22 (Mandy Moore) John Shearer/Wire Image/ Getty Images.

Library of Congress Cataloging-in-Publication Data

Koontz, Robin Michal.
  New Hampshire : the Granite State / Robin Koontz.
      p. cm. — (Our amazing states)
  Includes index.
  ISBN 978-1-4488-0648-5 (library binding) — ISBN 978-1-4488-0728-4 (pbk.) — ISBN 978-1-4488-0729-1 (6-pack)
  1. New Hampshire—Juvenile literature. I. Title.
  F34.3.K66 2011
  974.2—dc22
                                2009048628

Manufactured in the United States of America

CPSIA Compliance Information: Batch #WS10PK: For Further Information contact Rosen Publishing, New York, New York at 1-800-237-9932

Contents

A Land of Beauty

New Hampshire's beauty has **inspired** people for thousands of years. One well-known person it inspired was the poet Robert Frost. In 1923, his book of poems named after the state was published. New Hampshire still inspires people today. **Millions** of people visit it each year. Some visitors send postcards telling about their visits. Others take pictures of the state.

New Hampshire is in a group of six states called New England. It is in the northeastern part of the United States. New Hampshire's western border is the Connecticut River. Many of the state's hills and mountains are made of **granite**. Granite is a hard rock. New Hampshire has so much granite that its nickname is the Granite State.

New Hampshire has several dozen covered bridges, such as this one in Lincoln, New Hampshire. The roofs over these bridges keep them clear and safe in bad weather.

The Earliest People

People have lived in New Hampshire for many years. Stone tools that are thousands of years old were found near the state's Amoskeag Falls. By the 1600s, thousands of Native Americans lived there. The Abenakis and Pennacooks were the main Indian groups in the area. Many of them built homes called wigwams. They hunted and fished in the forests and rivers. They also grew crops.

In 1623, English people settled along the coast. They were sent by a man named John Mason. They caught fish to sell in England. In 1629, the settlements became the **colony** of New Hampshire. More settlers followed. Some traded with the Indians for furs and wood. They sold these in England, too.

Visitors to the Strawbery Banke Museum, in Portsmouth, New Hampshire, can learn about the past. Strawbery Banke was settled in 1630. It was one of the state's first English settlements.

Fighting for Success

In time, more settlers moved to New Hampshire. By the 1760s, many people in New Hampshire felt that they should no longer be ruled by the English. People in 13 other English colonies agreed. New Hampshire was the first colony to declare its **independence** from England. Other colonies soon followed. The English did not want to lose their colonies, though. They fought a war to try to hold on to them. However, the colonists won. They formed a new country, called the United States.

As part of this new country, New Hampshire kept growing. People built lumber mills and paper factories. The U.S. **Navy** built ships there. The first free public library was founded in Peterborough, New Hampshire, in 1833.

In the 1800s, New Hampshire had several textile mills, such as this one in Newport, New Hampshire. Textile mills are places where cloth is made.

A Pretty Cool Place

Hills, valleys, and mountains shape much of the beauty of New Hampshire. The middle of the state is part of the Eastern New England Upland. It has river valleys, hills, and lakes. The Merrimack River runs through this area. More rivers wind through southeastern New Hampshire. The White Mountains are in the northern part of the state. New Hampshire was once known for a rock formation called the Old Man of the Mountain. Sadly, this giant rocky face fell apart in 2003.

Summers in New Hampshire are most often pleasant and cool. Winter is very cold there. The state gets a lot of snow. The heavy snow makes New Hampshire a great place to ski.

Bretton Woods, in New Hampshire's White Mountains, is a well-liked skiing spot. The area also has great views of the beautiful White Mountains.

The Wild Woods

Most of New Hampshire is covered with trees and plants. Trees such as maples, oaks, and white birches grow in the forests. They are used to make all kinds of wood **products**. Plants such as blueberries also grow in the forests. Daisies, black-eyed Susans, and other colorful wildflowers dot the woodland fields in spring and summer.

The trees and bushes give many animals a safe place to live. There are black bears and moose in the thick forests of the north. Squirrels live in the trees. The shy white-tailed deer is the state animal. It likes to hide in wooded places. White-tailed deer will wave their tails if they are scared. They can run fast through the trees.

Adult male white-tailed deer grow a pair of antlers on their heads. They are large animals. An adult male white-tailed deer can weigh as much as 300 pounds (136 kg).

A Land That Gives Back

The millions of people who visit New Hampshire each year help the state's **economy**. People on vacation spend money! Visitors eat, shop, and stay in **hotels**. Some visitors even decide to buy land so that they can have a home in New Hampshire.

Many people have businesses in New Hampshire. Manufacturing, or making goods, is the biggest business there. Manchester and Nashua are cities by the Merrimack River in New Hampshire. These cities have factories that put together goods, such as computers and machine parts. In Nashua, people also make supplies for the U.S. **military**. New Hampshire produces a lot of lumber and other wood products, too.

Visitors to New Hampshire can pick apples and see apple cider being made. Cider is a drink made from pressed fruit. These people are making cider in Groveton, New Hampshire.

A Visit to Concord

Concord has been the capital of New Hampshire since 1808. The statehouse there was built from granite. The granite was mined from hills close by. Visitors can take tours of the big building.

Visitors to Concord can also tour the Pierce Manse. This big, old house was the home of Franklin Pierce. Pierce is the only person from New Hampshire to have become president of the United States. A group called the Pierce Brigade saved the house from being torn down.

People also like to visit the McAuliffe-Shepard Discovery Center in Concord. The center has a big **telescope** for looking at faraway planets and stars. It also has a **planetarium**. There, visitors can learn about space.

The New Hampshire Statehouse was built between 1816 and 1819. A statue of an eagle is on top of the building. A statue of the statesman Daniel Webster stands in front of it.

Mighty Mount Washington

New Hampshire's Mount Washington is the tallest mountain in the northeastern United States. It is in the White Mountains. Native Americans call it Agiocochook. This name means "home of the Great Spirit."

Visitors can ride up the mountain on a kind of train called a cog railway train. On top of the mountain, people can visit several buildings. One of the buildings is the Mount Washington **Observatory**. There, people study the weather. They record the weather year-round, no matter how bad it is. In 1934, the world record for the highest wind speed was set on Mount Washington. The wind blew at 231 miles per hour (372 km/h)!

Mount Washington's cog railroad has carried visitors up the mountain and above the clouds since 1869. It was the world's first mountain-climbing cog railroad.

Spending Time in New Hampshire

There is a lot to do in New Hampshire. The state has more than 60 state parks. Most of them have places to hike and camp. Some people hike through the state's Great North Woods. There, they can see moose! Climbers enjoy New Hampshire, too. Mount Monadnock is in southwestern New Hampshire. It is said to be the most climbed mountain in the United States. It has more than 40 miles (64 km) of trails.

New Hampshire has great places for fishing, swimming, and boating, too. There are hundreds of lakes there. In towns such as Hampton Beach, New Hampshire, people can swim in the ocean. New Hampshire is a fun place to visit. People love to live there, too!

Glossary

colony (KAH-luh-nee) A new place where people move that is still ruled by the leaders of the country from which they came.

economy (ih-KAH-nuh-mee) The way in which a country or business overseas its goods and services.

granite (GRA-nit) Melted rock that cooled and hardened beneath Earth's surface.

hotels (hoh-TELZ) Buildings with rooms that people pay to sleep in.

independence (in-dih-PEN-dents) Freedom from the control of other people.

inspired (in-SPY-urd) Moved someone to do something.

military (MIH-luh-ter-ee) Having to do with the part of the government, such as the army or navy, that keeps its citizens safe.

millions (MIL-yunz) Thousands of thousands.

navy (NAY-vee) A group of sailors who are trained to fight at sea.

observatory (ub-ZUR-vuh-tor-ee) A building in which scientists study the stars and the weather.

planetarium (pla-nih-TER-ee-um) A theater with a domed screen on top used for looking at pictures of the night sky.

products (PRAH-dukts) Things that are made.

telescope (TEH-leh-skohp) A tool used to make faraway objects appear closer and larger.

New Hampshire State Symbols

State Tree
White Birch

State Animal
White-Tailed Deer

State Flag

State Bird
Purple Finch

State Flower
Purple Lilac

State Seal

Famous People from New Hampshire

Franklin Pierce
(1804–1869)
Born in Hillsborough, NH
U.S. President

Alan Shepard
(1923–1998)
Born in East Derry, NH
Astronaut

Mandy Moore
(1984–)
Born in Nashua, NH
Singer and Actress

New Hampshire State Map

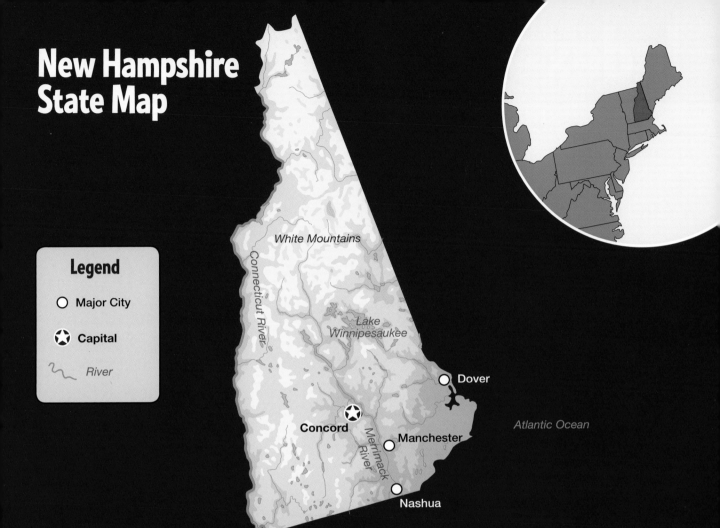

Legend

○ Major City

★ Capital

〰 River

White Mountains

Connecticut River

Lake Winnipesaukee

Dover

Concord

Manchester

Merrimack River

Atlantic Ocean

Nashua

New Hampshire State Facts

Population: About 1,235,786

Area: 9,279 square miles (24,032 sq km)

Motto: "Live Free or Die"

Song: "Old New Hampshire," words by John F. Holmes and music by
Maurice Hoffmann

Index

Web Sites

Due to the changing nature of Internet links, PowerKids Press has developed an online list of Web sites related to the subject of this book. This site is updated regularly. Please use this link to access the list:
www.powerkidslinks.com/amst/nh/